THEN &

C000027740

ST. CHARLES

Vicki Berger Erwin
and Jessica Dreyer

To our grandchildren, present and future, to remind them that their grandmothers made more than cookies.

—*VBE and JRD*

Copyright © 2011 by Vicki Berger Erwin and Jessica Dreyer
ISBN 978-0-7385-8352-5

Library of Congress Control Number: 2010937033

Published by Arcadia Publishing
Charleston, South Carolina

Printed in the United States of America

For all general information, please contact Arcadia Publishing:
Telephone 843-853-2070
Fax 843-853-0044
E-mail sales@arcadiapublishing.com
For customer service and orders:
Toll-Free 1-888-313-2665

Visit us on the Internet at www.arcadiapublishing.com

ON THE FRONT COVER: The Missouri Kansas Texas Railroad (MKT or "Katy") linked St. Louis and Kansas City as well as destinations south, passing through St. Charles. Shown here around 1900, the Katy opened in St. Charles in 1892 and closed in 1958. The depot was the site of a robbery and kidnapping on February 3, 1921, when five men robbed a U.S. mail messenger of money from five St. Charles banks and kidnapped him; he escaped. Originally located at the foot of Tompkins Street, the depot, after falling in serious disrepair, was relocated to Frontier Park and restored. Today the Katy Trail, built over the abandoned Katy roadbed, is a biking/hiking trail stretching across the state.

ON THE BACK COVER: The delivery wagon and horse stand ready at Brause's Grocery on the 800 block of Adams Street. It is one example of the many neighborhood groceries that once operated in St. Charles. Owner William Brause stands in the doorway in this photograph, along with (front row) Malinda Brause, Edna Brause, and William Brause; (second row) Julius Feldman, Walter Brause, Erna Brause, and Adele Brause.

CONTENTS

ACKNOWLEDGMENTS

We would like first and foremost to thank the St. Charles County Historical Society, who shared knowledge and photographs with us—especially archivist Bill Popp. Bill was unfailingly generous of his time and patience and always came up with the right photograph at the right time. Special thanks also goes to Cleta Flynn for her input and assistance.

When we began this project, we had no idea how many buildings had been altered, had disappeared, or had a change in address. We walked the bricks of Main Street in the rain and during one of the hottest summers on record to figure out the "now" buildings that matched with our "then" photographs. We hope we were right in our choices more times than not. And our respect for historians grew by leaps and bounds as our research sometimes uncovered not one date but as many as five dates for a building or event! It was a challenge to attempt to choose the "right" one, and right or wrong, it was entirely our choice.

Thanks to the preservation pioneers who so beautifully and lovingly restored the historic district. They deserve a huge round of applause for their efforts. For more information on this phase of St. Charles history, check out www.preservationjournal.org.

To Anna Wilson and John Pearson, as well as the proofreaders and copy editors at Arcadia Publishing, thank you, thank you—for your enthusiasm, answers to our silly questions, and wonderful attention to this project.

All "then" photographs are from the collection of the St. Charles Historical Society unless otherwise noted. All "now" photographs were taken by Jessica R. Dreyer unless otherwise noted.

To the employees at Main Street Books, I know I wasn't always as attentive to business as I should have been as the deadline for this book approached. Thanks for sticking it out and working so hard. Now go sell this book to the customers who have been asking for it for so long. I'd also like to thank my husband, Jim, and my family for all their support.

—VBE

A special thanks goes to my husband, John; my sons, Ed and Jim; and all my family and friends for their support during this project.

—JRD

INTRODUCTION

A stone marker at 906 South Main Street denotes the spot where Louis Blanchette, the first white man to settle in St. Charles, built his cabin in 1769. He had made an earlier reconnaissance trip along the Missouri River searching for a suitable location for a trading post, and upon his return, he chose Les Petite Cotes ("the little hills") because the river provided transportation, and fresh spring water was located nearby. Blanchette's wife, Angelique, came with him, as did several men who soon took Native American wives, started families, and created a community.

Although Blanchette and the settlers who arrived in St. Charles in those early days were French, they lived under the Spanish flag in what was called then San Carlos. Blanchette served as commandant until his death in 1793. In 1800, in a secret deal, France took control of the Louisiana territory—land west of the Mississippi River to the Rocky Mountains and from British America in the north to Mexico in the south—placing St. Charles under the French flag. That paved the way for the Louisiana Purchase, bringing St. Charles under a third flag, that of the United States, in 1803.

Meriwether Lewis and William Clark embarked upon their famous expedition from St. Charles on May 21, 1804. In the 35 years from Blanchette's arrival with his wife and handful of followers, Lewis and Clark reported St. Charles's population as 400 with 100 houses. The culture was predominantly French at that time; this is still evident in the restored architecture on Main Street and in the area dubbed Frenchtown.

After the Louisiana Purchase, pioneers from Kentucky, Tennessee, Virginia, and the Carolinas made the journey and settled in St. Charles, following the lead of Daniel Boone, who the Spanish lured to the area with a large land grant in 1799. St. Charles was an important point in journeys westward for many travelers, giving rise to businesses catering to these travelers.

In 1820, St. Charles had a population of approximately 1,200 citizens and was considered the population center of the state. During the state constitutional convention in St. Louis, delegates voted to make St. Charles the state capital upon Missouri's admission to the Union. That occurred on August 10, 1821, and St. Charles remained the capital until 1826.

An influx of German immigrants arrived in the second half of the 19th century in response to the German political situation and a handbook written by Gottfried Duden, widely read in Germany, touting the opportunity in Missouri and its similarity to their homeland. The new residents created a community characteristically German in architecture and lifestyle.

Throughout the shifts in population, Main Street continued to serve as the center of business and industry as well as residence. Industry, such as the American Car and Foundry, thrived. Population continued to grow before shifting westward.

By the 1960s, many of the Main Street buildings, including the structures used for the state capitol in the 1820s, were falling into disrepair. A group of forward-thinking citizens banded together to save the historic capital, and this led to the purchase and renovation of the buildings by the State of Missouri.

Success bred success, and the effort to preserve Main Street expanded into a study of the history and architecture of buildings along the street from Madison Street to Boone's Lick Road. This in turn led to the district being placed on the National Register of Historic Places in June 1970.

Federal money became available, and more and more buildings were renovated and turned into thriving businesses. The riverfront was cleaned up, and Frontier Park was born. Along Main Street, two small parks, Berthold Square and Kister Park, were created. Restoration spilled over to Frenchtown and the historic downtown area of North Main Street, with both being named to the National Register of Historic Places.

Not every building was preserved, and some of the photographs show that as well. St. Charles celebrated 200 years as an incorporated city in 2009, and thanks to the efforts of preservationists, some of the buildings on Main Street have also passed the bicentennial mark with others approaching that milestone. The city today is a model for preservation efforts, and citizens are justly proud of their history and the fact that they have visible proof of their city's past to show friends and neighbors.

HISTORIC
MAIN STREET

F. W. Woolworth's, seen here in the 1940s, was a popular five-and-dime store located at 229 North Main Street during the heyday of downtown North Main. Before it was a five-and-dime, the location was a hotel and after, Thro's, a local clothing store, has occupied the address.

German immigrants recognized St. Charles as an ideal location for grape growing and winemaking. A wine garden at 1219 South Main Street was established overlooking the Missouri River with this *c.* 1869 Swiss chalet–style building, shown here around 1900. For many years, the Wepprich family owned and operated the facility, selling it in 1973. Today the chalet still houses a restaurant, but the surrounding area has changed to include condominiums and parking lots.

James Mackay arrived in America from Scotland around 1776. In 1795, he led an expedition "to ascertain the discovery of the Pacific sea"—nine years before Lewis and Clark. He traveled approximately halfway to the Pacific Ocean. Mackay was named third commandant of San Carlos in 1801, serving until 1804 when the United States took possession. His home at 1017 South Main Street (above) was built around 1799 and dismantled in the 1950s. It was replaced by modern construction (below).

A hostelry popular with westbound travelers operated at 1001 South Main Street from around 1821. In 1864, August Blesse took over and named the business Western House (above). Stables, a wagon yard, and a blacksmith shop were located behind the main building, but they are no longer there. The business continued under Blesse's management for 18 years. In the 1950s, the building housed a corner market.

The structure, like many Main Street buildings, fell into disrepair and required renovation as seen in the photograph above, taken around 1976. Today Western House operates a retail establishment and as part of the Conservatory, a popular wedding site in St. Charles.

This Greek Revival structure, located at 1000 South Main Street and known originally as the Carter-Rice House, dates to 1832 (assessor) or 1840 (the Preservation Journal) and—as seen below—was seriously in need of saving in the late 1970s. Paul and V'Anne Mydler purchased the building in 1980 and spent six years restoring it. Today the building is a bed-and-breakfast.

In 1851 or 1852, Gibbs and Broadwater opened the St. Charles Woolen Mill, pictured above around 1890. The site previously hosted an early gristmill. During the Civil War, Union forces took possession and used the building as a prison for locals who refused to take an oath of allegiance to the U.S. government. After the war, several attempts to produce various products at the mill failed. The building was damaged by fire in 1966 but has been restored and operates as a restaurant.

The house at 906 South Main Street dates to 1850 (pictured above around 1940), but the site itself is where Louis Blanchette, founder of St. Charles, established his headquarters in 1769. He settled in Les Petite Cotes with his wife and several fur trappers to establish a trading post. Blanchette was the first Spanish commandant, serving until his death in 1793. A marker erected by the Daughters of the American Revolution (DAR) in 1921 commemorates the first settlers of St. Charles. The building is in use as a retail establishment.

Originally brick, this building at 903 South Main Street (seen below in the 1940s), is known as the Tiercerot House and was constructed in the French style around 1830 by Georgoire Tiercerot. The home was two and a half stories and had five rooms with access to the upper-level living quarters via an outside stairway. The brick has been covered with stucco and the building is in commercial use.

John Coontz built a one-room house at 119 McDonough around 1790. The land was acquired by the Tayon family, and Don Carlos Tayon, who served as the second commandant of San Carlos from 1793 to 1801, expanded the house. It is pictured below in the 1930s. The brick house rests on a stone foundation and is considered a prime example of French architecture. The house entertained such famous visitors as explorer William Clark (May 1804) and author Washington Irving (1832). The building is still in use.

Seen here in the late 1970s, the city garage was located at 812–828 South Main Street. It was where equipment and street salt were stored. New construction designed to fit the style of the old buildings replaced the garage. Retail and offices operate at this address today.

In 1807, David McNair, brother of Missouri's first governor, built the house at 724 South Main Street of handmade brick. An enterprising businessman who owned a limekiln and tan yard nearby, McNair also operated a ferry business, and it is thought that the house originally faced the river. Historians believe Lewis and Clark departed from the site where McNair would later establish his ferry landing on May 21, 1804. The vintage photograph above shows the house around 1936. Today it is a retail establishment.

Henry and John Schemmer operated a blacksmith shop at 709 South Main Street from the early 1890s. The building, seen below in the 1960s, is an example of German-influenced architecture, and the arches and cornices showcase the skills of German immigrant bricklayers. The arched door, which led straight through the building in wagon-making days, has been replaced by a fixed window in the structure's present incarnation as a retail shop. The Schemmers also built matching brick homes nearby for their families.

Seen here below 1976, the two-and-a-half-story brick structure at 701 South Main Street was built around 1801 as a customs house. Spain required all travelers and wagons to stop for an inspection and obtain a permit for their westward journey; they were not allowed to travel on Sundays. The third floor was used for overnight accommodations for human travelers, while a stable behind the building provided care for horses. The building houses a retail establishment today.

Around 1805, a French-influenced, two-and-a-half-story building was erected at 700 South Main Street with bricks fired on location. This structure was either replaced or greatly expanded in 1816. During St. Charles's first days as a capital city, the Farmers Tavern was popular with legislators. In 1856, when the photograph above was taken, new owners changed the building's name to Farmer's Home. Today the rehabbed structure houses retail shops on the ground floor and apartments above.

In 1838, Franklin Newbill created the basement and first floor of the Newbill-McElhiney House (625 South Main Street), seen above in the 1890s. In 1858, Dr. William McElhiney bought and enlarged the home to its present structure. McElhiney lived in the house with his wife and 14 children. The St. Charles County Historical Society purchased and rehabbed the home around 1971, using it as a headquarters until moving to its present location. Today the Newbill-McElhiney House is a private residence, museum, and retail shop.

Constructed around 1840, the small two-story brick building located behind the Newbill-McElhiney House at 621 South Main Street (seen below around 1976) is reputed to have been the living quarters for the family's enslaved servants until the Civil War. In more recent years, the house has been used as both a residence and retail store.

Around 1831, Catherine Collier, a widow, built what is believed to be one of the oldest brick churches west of the Mississippi River at 617 South Main Street. On weekdays, the building was a school, and on Sundays it served as a meeting place for several congregations. At the 10:00 am Methodist service, African American worshippers heard the same sermon as white congregants but from a separate room. In more recent years, the building has been a residence and a law office.

The exact date of the original building at 600 South Main Street is unknown, but in a March 1812 letter to his son in Ohio, Col. Timothy Kibby wrote that his home "on the corner of Main Street and Pike" had been damaged by the New Madrid earthquake. There is some question whether the current house (seen above in the 1950s) is the original or a newer one built on the same site. Today the location is a retail operation. ("Now" image, Vicki Berger Erwin collection.)

The building at 515 South Main Street looks little like the original two-story structure built in the early 1800s. Eckert's Tavern was extensively damaged in the tornado that struck St. Charles on February 26, 1876, and has been rebuilt. The eatery was a popular wagon stop on the way west. Maj. George Sibley of St. Charles and his team met at the Tavern to complete the final report on their mapping of the Santa Fe Trail in 1827. Today it is once again a dining establishment. (Drawing from the collection of Ryne Stiegemeier.)

Francis X. Kremer, a successful mill owner, built St. Charles's first double house at 500 South Main Street around 1860. It is seen below in the 1950s. Kremer's family lived on one side, and his mother-in-law inhabited the other. The two sides were said to be furnished exactly alike, but no door connected them from the inside. At one time, there was a double front door. Local folklore claims that the ghost of the mother-in-law haunts the home, which now operates as a restaurant.

The small house at 401 South Main Street is an excellent example of pioneer French architecture, seen here around 1960. Fr. Charles Van Quickenborne bought the property in 1818, and the building was erected around 1820 of handmade brick. It served as a rectory when priests were in St. Charles and also as an armory for the militia. The original St. Charles Borromeo Church and cemetery were located behind this building. The cemetery was relocated, and the church was reconstructed. The site is a retail space now.

A one-story brick building at 400 South Main Street housed the St. Charles Steam Laundry in the late 1800s when this photograph was taken. Today Albert F. Kister Park and Bandstand (commonly referred to as "the Gazebo") occupy the site. Kister was a civic leader and St. Charles's Man of the Year in 1960.

Joseph May built 337 South Main Street in 1870 to house his family and his marble and granite business. The Corinthian columns shown flanking the front entrance in this 1960s photograph (at right) were carved on the premises. The double front doors and sloping floor made it possible for May and his workers to roll finished pieces directly onto waiting wagons. A business operates at the address today.

The buildings at 314–324 South Main Street, shown below in the 1960s, are designated Stone Row because of their hand-cut Burlington limestone. Thomas Lindsay (Lindsey) erected the row around 1815. Some 40 years later, the brick building at 322 was added to what had formerly been an arched walkway. Probably the houses originally faced the river; this is suggested by the porches across the "backs" of the buildings. Businesses operated on the ground floor, and people lived above. Today the buildings are used in a variety of ways.

Seen below in the 1940s, California House Tavern at 315 South Main (built around 1820) is the last two-story log house in St. Charles, although it is now covered by clapboard siding. The tavern was a stagecoach stop as well as a gathering place for legislators when St. Charles was the state capitol. A part of the building was destroyed by the 1876 tornado and never replaced. The California Tavern is now a retail establishment.

William G. Pettus built his two-and-a-half-story brick home at 307 South Main Street in 1821 while serving as Missouri's secretary of state. He found the capitol buildings too crowded. Pettus was also secretary of the Missouri Constitutional Convention, and the state's original constitution is written in his hand. A fire destroyed the building in the early 1950s, and it has been rebuilt. The Main Cleaning Company (seen in the above photograph) called it home in the 1930s. Today it is a retail location.

Dr. Seth Millington built 301 South Main Street in 1799. Millington's niece married abolitionist and newspaperman Elijah P. Lovejoy, and while visiting the Millington home Lovejoy delivered an anti-slavery sermon at the Presbyterian church. According to local lore, an angry mob gathered outside the house, attempting to lynch Lovejoy. He escaped and made it to Alton, Illinois, where he was killed by a similar mob on November 7, 1837. Today the site is a long-established printing company ("Then" photograph from the collection of Bill Goellner.)

In 1855, Edward F. Gut constructed the three-story stone building at 300 South Main Street (seen below between 1900 and 1920). The first floor housed a business, and the upper floors were used as a residence. The hand-cut stone was numbered and notched to fit together. A cornerstone (dated 1855) is visible over the north front door of the second-floor porch. Joseph Jacob Seiling bought the building around 1880 and relocated his music store to the first floor. Now the location is a bar.

Berthold Park (on the northwest corner of Main and First Capitol/Clay Streets) was the site of the home of Maj. James Morrison around 1801. Morrison was a partner with two of Daniel Boone's sons in the salt business. The property was deeded to the city in 1974. Frederick Heye moved his tinsmith/hardware shop nearby to 217 South Main Street into a building dating to 1884. The Heye family continued to operate a business at the location until 1982. A restaurant operates there today.

Around 1822, John Mullanphy, St. Louis's first millionaire, gave his daughter Jane the Chambers Hotel as a wedding gift. It is seen above around 1920. The hotel did a brisk business when St. Charles was state capital, and its dining room was reputedly a favored eatery of Gov. Alexander McNair. The family sold the hotel in 1892 or 1893, and it became the Virginia Hotel. Through the years, the building also housed popular barbers and eating establishments. It was razed around 1967. Today the site is home to the St. Charles Tourism Center.

Seen above in the late 1800s, the three connected two-and-a-half-story buildings that housed the Missouri State Capitol were built around 1819. Brothers Ruluff and Charles Peck owned the buildings. Chauncy Shepard bought the northern section as a home. From 1821 to 1826, the Missouri General Assembly met on the second floor of the center and southern sections. Governor McNair's office was located on the second floor of the northern building. Businesses continued to operate on the ground floor. After the state capital moved to Jefferson City, the buildings reverted to their original business and residential uses.

The buildings fell into increasing disrepair until 1961, when interested citizens persuaded the State of Missouri to acquire the property and restore the buildings (seen above before their restoration).

Today the location is operated as a Missouri State Historical Site, and visitors are welcome to experience Missouri's first State Capitol as it was during those days.

A home belonging to Antoine Reynal originally occupied 119 South Main Street. From around 1848 to 1904, the St. Charles County Courthouse was located on this site. It is seen below in the 1850s. The building sustained damage in the cyclone of February 26, 1876, but not as much as the neighboring concert hall, which was completely destroyed. Reputedly, the Slave Block—a large flat stone at the right-front corner of the courthouse sidewalk—was used for slave auctions.

Post Office St Charles Mo.
Looking South West
Oct. 30-09.

However, during recent excavations no Slave Block was in evidence. A U.S. post office was built on the location of the old courthouse in 1904. Men gather on the post office steps in the above 1909 photograph. The post office moved to Fifth Street, and the building is now privately owned.

The building seen on the right in this 1920s image (above) began life as a public market and fish house around 1832 with scales for weighing produce and a public bulletin board as well as city offices. By the time of this photograph, the structure had undergone renovations and additions, including a major rebuilding project in 1886. St. Charles City Hall was housed in the building until 1973; the St. Charles County Historical Society now occupies the building. The neighboring structure dates to 1878 and has been used as a bank and Odd Fellows Hall. Today it is home to business offices.

Ludwig Meyer bought the lot at 101 North Main Street in 1838. At that time, it was occupied by a wood-frame house (below, lower left corner). He constructed a three-story brick building in 1864 (or 1859, in upper left corner) and ran his jewelry business on the ground level and lived above. The third floor was damaged beyond repair in the 1876 cyclone and never replaced. Meyer Jewelry continued as a family business on this site until 1966. Today a coffeehouse is located here.

BLT. 1859 PARTLY DES. TORNADO-1876

REBUILT - 1876 & REMODELED - 1896 & 1900.

THE OLD HOME

WHERE OUR PARENTS LIVED & DIED. THE SCENE OF OUR HAPPY CHILDHOOD DAYS, AND WHERE SO MANY YEARS OF OUR MATURE LIFE IN SORROW & JOY WERE SPENT.

BUILT - 1837 & TORN DOWN IN 1859

The building at 130 South Main Street was the home of A. R. Huning's Department Store (seen below around 1865) on the ground level and Rudolph Goebel's photography gallery on the second floor. The building's age is in question, with construction dates ranging from 1849 to 1880. Because Huning went off to fight in the Civil War, returning to the dry goods business after his service in 1862 or later, the date is probably somewhere in between. The building is now a restaurant.

The photograph above presents a view of Main Street looking north from the intersection of Main and Jefferson Streets in December 1949. Meyer Jewelry is the brick building on the left. Union Electric (UE) is on the right, and First National Bank (barred windows) is north of UE. In the "now" photograph, there are no electrical lines. Although the buildings still exist, they have been repurposed.

The First National Bank, seen here around 1890), was the first bank in St. Charles County organized under national banking laws (December 16, 1863). The bank survived tornadoes, Yankee looters, robbers, and takeovers, but eventually succumbed. Today the bank's vaults are visible to diners in the restaurant occupying 100 North Main Street.

In the 1970s, North Main Street was transformed into the pedestrian-only Riverside Mall as shown in this 1983 photograph (below). The idea proved unpopular, and today historic downtown's brick streets are open to vehicular traffic.

Dr. Henry Behrens constructed the one-story brick building seen in this undated photograph (below) and practiced medicine at the site for several years. By some reports, Dr. Behrens's practice began in 1850; others claim that he started as early as 1812. Orville Denning and Saul Wolff erected the present building in 1946. Wolff started Standard Drug, which expanded to several St. Charles locations. Denning operated an appliance store and the Record Bar. Doctors and dentists rented the second floors. It is an office building now.

The location 126–130 North Main Street has enjoyed a varied history. From 1851 to 1885 (alternate date 1890), Adam Klinger operated St. Charles City Mills, one of three flour mills on Main Street. Theodore Klinger built the present structure around 1896. George Barklage and Louis Ringe Jr. purchased the building and sold farm machinery, surreys, and automobiles at the location from 1906 to 1936. The site later hosted a J. C. Penney, seen at left around 1976. It continues as a retail establishment today.

Seen above in the 1940s, the three-story brick building at 201–203 North Main Street was constructed in 1867 by German immigrant Francis Oberkoetter. His son-in-law operated the Mackenzie Hotel until 1894, when he sold it to H. B. Denker; Mackenzie was rumored to have to sell to settle gambling debts. In 1927, Huning Dry Goods moved to this location and continued in business until 1994. The Masonic Temple also occupied the upper levels. A restaurant occupies the ground floor today.

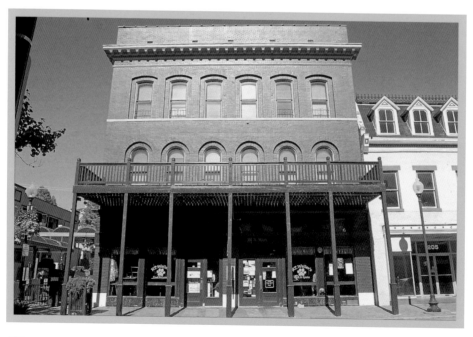

Seen at left in an undated photograph, the building at 208 North Main Street dates to 1904 and replaced an earlier structure from the mid-1800s. The shop sports pressed-metal ornamental cornices over a full glass front, glazed-brick piers, and a color tile entry. John Schulze was a pioneer in plumbing and sewers in St. Charles. In addition to residential work, he worked on plumbing for schools, banks, manufacturing, and St. Joseph's Hospital. The building is now home to a bar and grill.

The *Democrat* referred to in the building name, seen here around 1900, was a weekly German newspaper founded in 1852. The paper was also, at that time, Democratic politically. The newspaper was widely circulated and respected and had the strongest German voice outside of St. Louis. The site also was host to retail, medical, and apothecary businesses. Today it is a privately owned business office. ("Now" photograph from the collection of Vicki Berger Erwin.)

The original business housed at 229 North Main Street (shown above in the 1890s) was the New York Hotel, established around 1863. Expected patronage was interrupted by the Civil War, and it was sold and renamed Hoffman House in 1866. After tenure as a boardinghouse, the building was remodeled and reduced to two stories. It housed F. W. Woolworth's Five-and-Dime until the 1970s, when Thro's, a longtime St. Charles haberdasher, relocated to the site. It is still operating there today.

Seen here around 1900, Edward and John H. Steinbrinker operated their furniture and undertaking business from this location, 301–305 North Main Street, at the turn of the last century. Their undertaking services, including a casket, embalming, and grave digging, cost $123. Nowadays, a bar operates on the ground floor with offices overhead.

John Mittelberger built 311 North Main Street around 1870, although some historians date the original as late as 1880, to house an opera house on the second floor and his dry goods business on the ground floor. A fire in 1881 caused massive damage and the opera house, seen at left around 1910, was rebuilt. Theatergoers entered on Main Street and climbed stairs to the second-floor ticket office. Seating was available for 350 patrons. Today a banquet facility operates on the ground level with two floors of offices above.

The building at 340 North Main Street has met with more than its share of disaster. Dating to the mid-1800s, the building was originally a hotel. The Galt House, as it was known then, was damaged by a cyclone in 1902 (at right). In June 1935, railroad cars escaped the Wabash station, crashed into a bridge, and then into the Galt House (above). A 40-foot section of the bridge fell onto Main Street—fortunately without fatalities.

The building was remodeled after the hotel closed, and it was the home of the *St. Charles Banner*, a local newspaper (seen above around 1966). Today it houses a popular local pizza restaurant.

Building for the Steel Plant. July. 28. 1909.

The Foundry, originally home to the American Car and Foundry, initially produced railroad freight cars before expanding to trolleys, passenger cars, and custom coaches. During the World Wars, production switched to military equipment. The plant was one of the main employers in St. Charles before closing. Today one of the buildings is the Foundry Art Centre, an excellent example of repurposing. The center provides studio space for artists, exhibits, education, and performances of visual and performing arts.

OUT AND ABOUT ST. CHARLES

This view at the foot of Lewis Street at Main Street around 1887 shows the former St. Charles Borromeo Parochial residence after it had been turned into a boys' school. The buildings were dismantled to make room for the car foundry. At that time, Lewis Street cut through the middle of the current locations of Academy of the Sacred Heart and St. Charles Borromeo.

St. Charles is the county seat of St. Charles County, organized in 1812. The courthouse (second for the county) was constructed from 1901 to 1903. On the lawn is a marker designating the starting point of the Boonslick Trail. The building has been the scene of many special events, including the centennial celebration in 1909 (below). The courthouse is still in use as executive offices. A new facility houses other county functions and is located at 201 North Second Street.

This building (pictured above in the 1930s) was constructed at Second and Adams Streets in 1913 to serve as a streetcar terminal for both passengers and freight. The last streetcar left St. Charles on January 18, 1932. The terminal was a bus depot for a while and now houses a private business.

According to *McElhiney's Guidebook to Historic St. Charles, Missouri*, the stone home formerly located at 701 North Second Street was reputedly built around 1797 by Pierre Rondin, a "Free Negro" (one of four African Americans in the settlement) living in St. Charles. The founder of Chicago, Illinois, Jean Baptiste Point DuSable, gave the home to his granddaughter, along with the rest of his fortune, in return for caring for him during his last days. Alexander McNair, Missouri's first governor, also owned/resided in the home during his tenure. Shown at right in the 1880s, the building was razed around 1928. Today a business occupies the site.

In 1880, the building (seen below around 1900) at 1121 North Second Street housed Hose Company No. 2, a volunteer brigade. The fire alarm bell called the firemen when needed. The structure was converted to business use around 1943. Today it houses the Frenchtown Heritage Museum and Research Center. Frenchtown is an area of St. Charles—a city within a city in the mid-1800s—named to the National Register of Historic Places in 1991.

Catherine Collier and her sons, George and John, founded St. Charles College in the early 1830s. Classes were held in a temporary location until the building at 117 South Third Street (seen below around 1886) was completed in 1839. Classes were suspended during the Civil War, when the building was used as a hospital and prison. In 1891, the college moved into a new building farther west and operated until 1922. The old St. Charles College is now apartments.

Old St. Charles College, 1886, St. Charles, Mo.

When American Presbyterians split into Northern and Southern factions in 1861, two Presbyterian churches appeared in St. Charles. The church pictured at left (around 1900) was at the corner of Fifth and Madison Streets. It was two stories tall, with an auditorium on the second floor and Sunday school on the first. The church was later demolished to make way for the new post office.

Shown above in an undated photograph, the home at 305 Chauncey Street was built in 1836. Its second owners, Franz and Joanna Schulte, donated the home to St. Peter's Church around 1885, contingent upon the nuns opening a hospital there. The Sisters of St. Mary operated a 20-bed hospital until 1891, when the home reverted to residential use. A new hospital building was erected at 218 Clay (now First Capitol) Street in 1891, seen below around 1920. (From the collection of Ryne Stiegemeier.)

St. Joseph's Hospital, now known as SSM St. Joseph's Health Center, has experienced much expansion since its humble beginnings, including the one above pictured around 1960. Today the health center boasts 364 beds and almost 1,300 employees. It is home to the SSM Heart Institute, Center for Sleep Disorders, Cancer Care, and Vascular Institute, and it is a level II trauma center.

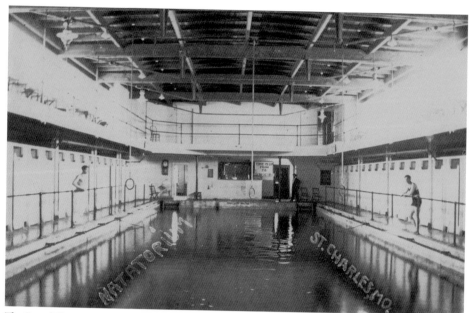

The Strand Theater operated at 220 North Second Street, bringing vaudeville, then silent movies, and then talkies to St. Charles residents (seen below around 1918). Note the advertising posters displayed in front of the theater. In an unusual move, the top floor of the theater was removed and replaced by a swimming pool (seen above around 1920). The Strand offered shows in winter and swimming in summer.

The building reverted to a cinema only and was known as St. Charles Cinema (seen above around 1974). The cinema was demolished and now the block is dominated by the new St. Charles City Hall and garage. ("Now" photograph from the collection of Vicki Berger Erwin).

Lindenwood College was founded as a girls' school in 1827 by Maj. George Sibley and his wife, Mary. The student body remained small, and the girls studied in log buildings as shown in the c. 1850 drawing seen above. In 1853, the Sibleys turned the school over to the St. Louis Presbytery, and it became Lindenwood Female College. Today the 15,000 students-strong coeducational institution is known as Lindenwood University.

The pillars marked the entrance to Lindenwood College for many years, as shown in the 1890 photograph below. A new entrance for Lindenwood University opened in 2010.

Lindenwood was originally located in a linden wood (hence the name) about a mile west of downtown. The secluded school has expanded, as has the surrounding neighborhood and city. The undated picture below shows the sparsely built neighborhood north of Lindenwood campus. The above image shows how it has built up. ("Now" photograph from the collection of Vicki Berger Erwin).

In 1818, when Sr. Philippine Duchesne arrived in St. Charles to start a school, conditions were harsh. Food and money were scarce, and the winter was bitter. That school did not survive, and Duchesne moved on to open two schools in St. Louis before returning to St. Charles in 1826 to reopen a school. Mother Duchesne is recognized as the founder of the worldwide Sacred Heart Schools. The photograph above shows the school grounds around 1930.

The chapel and the shrine to St. Philippine Duchesne are often confused. Adding to the confusion is the fact that originally St. Charles Borromeo Church was located on the present grounds of Academy of the Sacred Heart. The chapel is seen above around 1940.

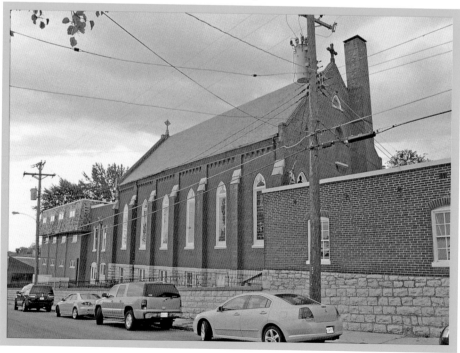

William H. Hall operated Boone's Lick Trading Post at 323 South Boone's Lick Road (shown below). The location was along the Old Plank Toll Road, which was a failed attempt to provide mud-free travel along planks laid out to form a road. The enterprise didn't succeed because wagons traveled alongside the planks to avoid the toll and settlers used the planks for firewood. A business occupies the site today.

The 1920s image and modern-day photograph of 203 Boone's Lick Road contrast the road conditions experienced then with those enjoyed now.

The St. Charles Military School was built at the corner of Sixth and First Capitol (Clay) Streets around 1860. The grounds included stables for students' horses. The school closed at the end of the Civil War, and Herman Bruns turned it into the Washington House Hotel around 1875 (seen above in an undated photograph). Today it is a bar, and the basement is the longtime home to cocked hat bowling, a three-pin game.

St. Charles Borromeo is the third-oldest parish in the St. Louis Archdiocese. The first church, San Carlos Borromeo, was located behind 401 South Main Street, where a replica church now stands (seen below). The building is of French *poteaux en terre* (vertical post in ground) style. Lewis and Clark's men celebrated Mass at this church. A second church was built in 1828 at Second Street and Decatur. In 1869, a third church was built on the present site, and it suffered great damage in the tornado of 1915.

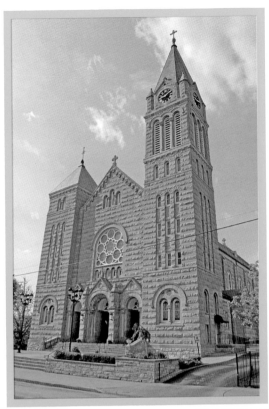

The cornerstone for the existing church was laid on April 16, 1916, by Card. John Glennon, and the church continues at that site today. The photograph below shows the rebuilding nearly complete in 1917.

St. Charles County has had six jails since 1804. The first jails operated on Main Street starting out at 514 South Main and moving to Stone Row during the town's days as state capital. From 1832 to 1876, the city and county operated a jail at Main and Pike Streets. A facility was then built at Second and Madison Streets. In 1911, the fifth jail (pictured below) was built at 120 South Second Street, housing 44 prisoners. A modern facility opened on January 7, 1989, and can host 324 prisoners.

OUT AND ABOUT ST. CHARLES

The A&W Root Beer stand, with its 5¢ root beer served in glass mugs, was a popular spot in St. Charles. In photograph above, taken around 1954, a large truck is too close for comfort to the parking awning and is the amusement of female onlookers. The building has been remodeled into a different business.

The first city library opened in 1914 in one room of the high school and continued there until 1931. There was no funding beyond donations until 1928, when a city library tax passed. The library then secured the building at 572 Jefferson Street. Because of her devoted service, the new building (seen above in the 1950s) was named for Kathryn M. Linnemann, the library's first librarian. In 1973, the city and county libraries merged, and one of the branches is still named after Linnemann.

The 1950s photograph below and the image above show the advancement in facilities at the Linnemann Library, now located at 2323 Elm Street. In addition to the Kathryn Linnemann Library, the St. Charles City County Library District has two additional regional branches with larger collections and subject specialists, four general branches, two library express branches, and three mini-branches. The district is one of the three most heavily used library districts in the state of Missouri.

Residents of St. Charles paid a tax as early as 1836 for fire-protection equipment. At that time, firefighters were volunteers with buckets. Hand-pulled wagons were the next step, followed by horse-drawn wagons (seen below in an undated photograph). Today firefighters operate out of five stations with the latest equipment, including five advanced life-support (ALS) engines, two ALS ladder trucks, four ambulances, one brush truck, one hazardous materials truck, and one rescue boat. The average arrival time for a call is four minutes.

CHAPTER

THE RIVERFRONT

The depot served the MKT Railroad in St. Charles from 1892, but when rail service declined the station closed and fell into disrepair. When the station (located at the foot of Tompkins Street) was slated for demolition to make way for Riverside Drive, the South Main Street Preservation Society stepped up and campaigned to save this example of Victorian railroadiana. With a community block grant, the station, shown here in 1976, was moved to Frontier Park and restored (see cover).

As illustrated in this undated photograph above, for many years riverboats plied the Missouri River, delivering goods and passengers to the St. Charles shore. In 1994, a different kind of riverboat docked in St. Charles—a riverboat casino. Initially Missouri casinos were required to be based on a boat that cruised the river, but that requirement was amended to allow land-based structures surrounded by a moat (commonly known as "boat in a moat"). Ameristar is such a casino on the St. Charles riverfront today.

In the summer of 1993, St. Charles was plagued by floodwaters. The photograph below gives a taste of the extent of flooding along the riverfront. It shows how high the water reached in the area surrounding the Jaycee stage in Frontier Park in July 1993. The above photograph is the pavilion under normal river conditions.

In these photographs of the view of the Missouri River from the old courthouse, it is possible to see the building and population growth in St. Charles City between the 1920s and today.

In the undated photograph above, a Boy Scout troop performs riverside. Could they be the ancestral inspiration of today's Lewis and Clark Fife and Drum Corps? Fife and Drum was founded in 1992 and features young people 10 to 18 years of age playing replica fifes and rope-tension drums as used during the 18th and 19th centuries. When performing, the corps wears red wool coats and bearskin-crested hats patterned after uniforms worn by U.S. Army field musicians from 1804 to 1810.

The St. Charles Municipal Band performs at Blanchette Park in 1934 photograph seen above. The 30-person band was officially established on April 8, 1929, in a city election. Entrance into the band was competitive and members received a small stipend. It was required to give 12 concerts per year and could be called upon to perform by the mayor. The city funding ceased in 1992. The band reorganized and continues to perform summer concerts (alternating with the Community Big Band) in Frontier Park with support from donations.

Since the town is located on the Missouri River, bridges have long been an important part of the St. Charles landscape. One of the first was a pontoon bridge that came to be called "Enoch's Folly." Devised by Capt. John Enoch, 50 barges floating on pontoons 26 feet by 10 feet in size were strung together with rope; the middle barges could be parted to allow boats to pass. The bridge opened on June 1, 1890, and closed in November 1890 when ice blocks smashed the barges. Today several modern bridges span the river linking west and east.

www.arcadiapublishing.com

Discover books about the town where you grew up, the cities where your friends and families live, the town where your parents met, or even that retirement spot you've been dreaming about. Our Web site provides history lovers with exclusive deals, advanced notification about new titles, e-mail alerts of author events, and much more.

Find Your Place in History.